SURRENDER
TO LIFE

Frederick D. Clark

ISBN: 1981468056
ISBN 13: 9781981468058

SUMMARY OF BOOK

The journey of a seventeen year old through his early years into the last 20 years that has taken him inside the PRISON WALLS to make a difference in the lives of thousands of inmates as well in himself.

This Book is part of the Non-Profit Ministry known as The Shepherd's Ministry of LaPine, Oregon, established in 2005 and opened up in 2006 as a Ministry that brings hope to the incarcerated.

Our mailing address is The Shepherd's Ministry
P.O. Box 3336
LaPine, Oregon 97739

ABOUT THE COVER

The title "Surrender To Life" expresses my beginning of walking with the Lord. My surrender in April 1964 was the true beginning of real-life for me. Life is what I signed up for when I surrendered to the Lord.

The man, an inmate, standing on the yard with his hands on a wall was a position I witnessed many times. Men would be put "on the wall" to be patted down or to be searched for contraband. This assumed position was a form of submission by the inmate.

I was sitting on the front row of a church where I was about to speak. The Lord let me see, I think in a vision, a man dressed in a black and white striped prison uniform, standing in front of the cross that was on the back wall of the platform. The man, had his arms on the Cross exactly like I had seen many times on the yard wall. I understood from this vision that God was showing me men who would surrender to the Cross that were incarcerated. I have seen this surrender many times. This surrender is to be for life. My life has been from surrender to life as I have understood the desire of the Lord Jesus Christ.

FORWARD AND ACKNOWLEGMENT

Some books have **Acknowledgments**. Other books have **Forwards**. I decided since this is my book I'm going to have the Forward and the Acknowledgments together. Besides all writers need to provide some opportunity for complaining for those who read the book with great skepticism

Forward: Sounds like a command that I use to hear when I was in the Army. It meant onward. In the books that I scanned looking at Forwards it seemed they were all written by someone that the Author could get to complement his work. Very few have read this before it came to print, so I don't have a lot of individuals to draw from that will compliment me. Of course my wife would but she declined.

Acknowledgments: I do have a number of individuals to acknowledge that have believed in me and the Ministry that I have brought into a life journey. It is a Ministry that, in the latter years and currently is, a Ministry that has reached inside a number of prisons both in California and more so in Oregon.

Rev. Sam Huddleston who wrote the book" 5 Years to Life" was one of the first individuals I shared with concerning my call into the prison. He understood this mission was a worthy mission and gave me great encouragement. In fact, on a couple of occasions, I sat at a table with several men who were Residents of The Shepherd's Ministry Home and Pastor Sam, on the speakerphone, would talk to the men around the table. How many people would do that? Each resident had to read his book before the call.

Chaplain Tim Woods was the first Prison Chaplain in Oregon, at Snake River Correctional Institution, in Ontario, that allowed me to speak and share The Shepherd's Ministry. It was at the gate that I discovered not only was he the Chaplain but I had been his Christian Education Pastor at Willamette Christian Center in Eugene when he was a young boy attending there with his parents.

Chaplain Ken Ball will probably be the last Prison Chaplain I will work under. He currently allows me to preach a Chapel Service once a month and a weekly Bible Study. He is my friend and a great encouragement.

Rev. Henry Porter a Deschutes County volunteer at the County Jail was one, in the early years I spoke with concerning the creation of The Shepherd's Ministry. He is a wonderful brother who gives himself to the incarcerated.

Rev. Ted Gibson, Former Pastor of the Assemblies of God Church in LaPine. Not only has he been my friend but he encouraged me early on.

Rev. Rance Kinser from Boring, Oregon has been my friend long before we moved to LaPine. He encouraged me to do what was in my heart. He Pastored Living Word Fellowship until his retirement. We are best Pastor friends to this day.

Rev. Lloyd Reece, is a long time friend from California and Oregon. I will never forget his efforts to always push me forward. What a friend he has been.

There have been many donors who have been with me from the beginning. Never missing a month in their giving to this Ministry. Mentioning names here may be embarrassing but certainly worthy of recognition. **Frank and Susan**, **Mike**, **Helen**, **Dave and Sherry**. Many others have given that has allowed me to continue this Ministry. The cost of men in the home, rent, utilities, food, vehicles, gas, and much more has been shared by all donors whether it was an one-time gift or ongoing. I can't list everyone but I acknowledge them and God knows who they are, too.

Rev. God, because without Him none of this would have happened. He says that he will supply all the necessary items that we need according to His riches in heaven. He has given them to us from His Cattle on a Thousand Hills, one hamburger at a time.

CONTENTS

CHAPTER ONE

THE VOYAGE

Pam and I went on a voyage to Alaska. It began at a Port which was the starting point. Our starting point of this voyage started in April, 1964. Our Alaskan voyage ended but my written voyage continues to my last breath.

1

"IN THE BEGINNING GOD CREATED"

Genesis 1:1

This is how this voyage began. In April 1964 I began my walk with Christ. That choice brought me to this time in my life. I didn't know then but that decision would effect the rest of my life. I am constantly teaching that the decision of yesterday will effect our today and the today decisions will effect our tomorrow.

I am sure that God had been tugging on my heart for some time prior to that day that found me sitting in a Study Hall Classroom at Lakewood High School in Lakewood, California. I certainly did not want to surrender, as I knew the cost of being a follower of this Jesus of Nazareth. From day one I knew the cost. It was ALL.

I never heard the song as "surrender part". My parents were not part-time Christians or Sunday Christians and my heritage was that of a Mom and Dad who were committed to Christ. As a result of this modeling from Sunday School Teachers, Pastors and Parents, my 17-year-old heart knew that to serve Jesus was a lifelong surrender - it was a "I surrender all".

Can a teenage kid surrender? Can a teenage kid run the race to the end? I remember on that special day in April saying "I give up Jesus, come into my heart". He did and my voyage took on a new course. That night I kneeled at my bed and prayed again. I prayed that Christ would come into my life. He was there and had been there for a few hours but I thought maybe "study hall" was not the place to be" born again". I was extremely serious about this commitment and wanted it to be right. My seriousness caused me to tell the Lord that "Father, even if Billy Graham backslides, I will serve you".

I know now that I didn't impress God but as I look back to that day and moment of change-I was serious! I understood that Christ requires placing father, mother, wife, children, brothers, sisters in second place to him.*

I still believe this today it has been 43+ years and I'm still on the voyage. I have not jumped ship, fell off the wagon, but followed through on my prayer to God that I will serve him to the end. Where is the end? If I get this book completed it will be after that.

---

* Matthew 10:37; Luke 14:26

In the beginning when God created in me a new heart as He said He would: "I will give them a heart to know Me... And I will give them one heart... And take the stony heart out of their flesh, and give them a heart of flesh".* I desired to run the race, finish the course and come face-to-face with the Father and have Him say:

"well done, good and faithful servant. **

There will be no almost well done. There will be no you almost placed me first. No, I kind of surrendered or I surrendered half the time.

The voyage of the believer is from the beginning to the end. It is from the port of departure to the port of arrival.

Anything short of a finished voyage is incomplete.

In a devotional I read "all voyages, those that are in waters we never sailed before, are full of uncertainty".

Every day brings waters never sailed before but there is a certainty that God is there. God is in my yesterday, my today and certainly my tomorrow. That is because my yesterday determines my today and my today will determine my tomorrow.

Your voyage like mine is a daily one. It begins as we rise and ends as we retire. I have determined, with God's help, to allow the hours between the two, to be filled with commitment and surrender.

---

* Jeremiah 24:7; Ezekiel 11:19

** Matthew 25:21

My voyage has taken me from Study Hall to the Army, to College, to Ministry and now into the last part of the voyage. In each of these parts of my life, I have remained faithful.

It was less than 30 days after my surrender that I found myself in the Army. I didn't know that this three year experience would be a vital part of my Voyage. It was a sink or swim experience. I had never sailed in this water before but I had made a commitment. This commitment caused me to be alone a lot. As the GI's went to the bars and party places, I went to the Day Room and developed my friendship with Jesus. Often I felt alone and indeed was alone but the commitment and the surrender kept me on course. After all, I was headed towards the Port of Arrival and today, I still am.

In the Day Room I would study the Word and work on the Bible Study Course that my Sunday School Teacher, Ned and Thelma, paid for and sent to me. What an interesting change that was. I wasn't very nice in my pre-voyage life. My Sunday School Teacher should have kicked me out of Sunday School for my disruptive behavior. Instead he just loved and tolerated me and then paid for the study material. I didn't deserve his kindness but he just prayed and kept teaching me. He has finished his voyage and has received his "well done". As I think about it, I didn't deserve a new heart but I received one.

The three years in the Army were initial years of growing. I began the development of my Christian life to be.

Several things took place and developed strengths in my Christian development. In Basic Training I began memorizing Scripture verses. The organization called the "Navigators", out of Colorado had a study for memorizing Scripture. I think it was called the Topical Memory Verse Program. I began to practice the Scriptures. and the Scripture that says "Thy Word have I hid in my heart that I might not sin against God" * and "Thy Word is a lamp unto my feet and a light to my path".** I not only memorized dozens and dozens of Scripture verses but believed them and set out to live them out.

It was in Basic Training that my Mom and Dad came to Monterey, California and I experienced my first weekend pass. We went to church and the Church, that Sunday, had Communion. My first Communion! My first Communion with my Mom and Dad. A special moment. I was about eight weeks old as a Christian but the **RACE WAS ON**. I didn't know much but I had made the declaration that I would run the race to the end. Some may think I was crawling. Some in a baby walk. Others in a run. Whichever one it was I was moving in the Kingdom of God on earth. God was there, holding my hand and walking out ahead of me.

Every time I could attend the Base Chapel, I would. While at Fort Sam Houston, Texas, I would attend at the Base Chapel and also I attended a church off-base. There

---

* Psalm 119:11

** Psalm 119:105

was a Servicemen's Center which was in downtown San Antonio by Fort Sam Houston. They served cookies and milk to the servicemen who would come off the street. Their mission was to share Christ with the servicemen. I learned a lot of new things there about my faith in Christ.

While in Vietnam, as a Combat Medic, I was part of the First Infantry Division and was assigned to an Engineer Battalion. I spent most of my time in the field. Our Engineer Battalion built landing zones in order for the Infantry to drop in and the helicopters to drop off food supplies. The Engineers were also involved in building bridges and mine sweeping. So whenever they went to the field to do one of these tasks I would go with them as their medic. It certainly was an interesting job as I was still a youngster myself at the age of 19. Being away from the Base Camp I was unable to have a Chapel to go to, so my Chapel became reading the Word and on Sundays I would sit on top of a tank [an APC) with my three band radio and up the antenna to listen to Christian stations that would come into Vietnam.

On one particular Sunday I heard a broadcast that was led by Dr. C.M. Ward that was called Revivaltime. The broadcast caught my attention immediately and I discovered at the end of that program, Dr. C.M. Ward and Revivaltime were part of the Assemblies of God coming out of Springfield, Missouri. All I know is that it fed my spirit and every Sunday thereafter, I would tune in to Revivaltime on my Three Band Radio. I remember writing a letter to Dr. C.M. Ward and believed that he personally sent me a letter. How important it was for me to receive a personal letter from this radio Evangelist who was sharing the Word with the soldiers in Vietnam. As a 19-year-old I conducted a Bible study out in the field and also back at the Base Camp. All I knew was that the Lord had saved me and I wanted to spread the Good News of the Christ I was serving.

I really don't remember much about these studies but I remember I did my best. I've always felt that the Word of God is important in our life if we are going to walk out our faith. I could tell many stories that came out of my experience in Vietnam but this book really is not about Vietnam other than it was part of my journey. In fact it was part of my early journey. I served three years in the Army and was discharged in 1967. I went in the Army as a Christian and I came out as a Christian because of my surrender and commitment in between the two. As others drank and lived their own lives, I followed through on my commitment to the Lord. I guess a kid can be committed.

Oh how I wanted to receive the "well done". I can see that the decision in 1964 to 1967 has determined my today.

In 2005 while preaching at the Chapel at Salinas Valley State Prison in Soledad, California in 2005 I had an inmate come to me after the Chapel Service and told me that I was his Teacher and Royal Ranger Commander in 1967. I came out of the Army serving and still in love with Christ and continued my walk by sharing my life with others. David was one I shared with. As David and I discovered each other, after 38 years, standing at the Altar Area

of the Prison Chapel – I realize that our decisions of yesterday really do effect our today (and tomorrow). That day
I left the prison and walked out and David had 14 years
to serve behind the bars. The next week as we met again,
David said "I should have listened to you the first time". My
response was "you're right". I love David. We wrote to each
other and he has completed many Bible Study Courses
since incarcerated and understands that his choices today
will determine his tomorrows. I hope we will meet outside
the prison gate. * At the end our voyage we will meet in
the presence of the Lord if we faint not. I'm still shooting
for the "well done".

In 1967 I began my pursuit of formal Bible Training
in the Southern California area. I attended Southern
California College, now known as Vanguard University
located in Costa Mesa. I also studied at L. I. F. E. Bible
College in Los Angeles. As I continued to commit myself to this new heart voyage I was "learning of Him".
Commitment and surrender will cause us to run into the
embrace of Christ.

Whatever we commit and surrender to is where we will
run. The Voyage continues to this day as I love the Words
of Christ. I love His teachings. I love His love. The person
we love, we will seek. Christ has told us to "seek first the
Kingdom of God..." **

---

* Today David is out of Prison on Parole. He lives in the Van
Nuys Area of Southern California

** Matthew 6:33

During my College Years I also served as a Youth Pastor. I didn't know much but I gave it my best. It was part of my Voyage and part of my today.

I taught a lot of youth in those years. I'll never know the impact I had on them, I'll never know the individuals who have maintained their commitment but God does. He keeps a record. He will speak the "well done". He will be at the Port of Arrival. What will God say to you? The rest of your life will end at the Port of Arrival.

My commitment and surrender is just that – it is mine. No one will create my Voyage. It is created as I live out my commitments. That is not overly profound, but true.

CHAPTER TWO

LOOKING BACK

The Apostle Paul said that we should forget those things that are behind and look forward to the things that are ahead. I believe this Inspired Word. I also believe there is a value in viewing the past. Memorials were made throughout the Old Testament for the purpose of remembering.

2

Looking back is a wonderful experience for me. It is in looking back that I reaffirm my future. I see the handprint of God in my life. As I walked in the past, I didn't have a clue, yet it is very clear today. Today I see the years of my 20s, 30s, and 40s as years of preparation for the 50 years and beyond.

I am reminded of the 40 years in the desert of the Israelites (yet I do not consider my years as being in the desert). The Apostle Paul experienced years of being taught by Christ. Certainly the Apostles looked back at their walk with Christ as they viewed their final days before their martyrdom.

My past hasn't been much except for the fact, it is mine and God created mine for me and the current day that He has brought me too.

In 1967 upon release from the military I knew that God wanted me to have formal Bible Training. So as a

20-year-old I entered college and with that came counseling at Youth Camps in the School of Evangelism that took me to the streets and exposure to the counterculture of the drug life. The drug culture of the late 60s, as youth were into heroin, acid, and other drugs that I knew nothing about. I never did drugs or alcohol because I had chosen three years earlier to do "Jesus".

In 1990 there was a moment in my journey I will never forget. My oldest brother Joe, four years older than I, placed himself into the Clint Eastwood Rehabilitation Center for his alcohol addiction. On the last week of his program I was called and asked if I would come and be with him and participate in a family session that was part of his program. I did. That session changed me and my relationship with Joe. Joe changed and has grown from that day to current. For 35 years alcohol embraced his life and the year from 1990 to current have been alcohol free. In 1990 after returning to his job and home, he began to watch the 700 club with Pat Robertson and had a life-changing experience with Christ. The Rehab Center introduce Christ and the 700 Club invited Joe to the Cross. Bottom line to all of this is that God "Restores what the locust has eaten* and He turns our mourning into joy.**

As I returned from this time with my brother, I cried like a baby for a long time. As I write this I can tell you that the years following the 1990 moment have been

---

* Joel 2:25
** Jeremiah 31:13

wonderful and the once distant relationship has not only been erased but a wonderful big brother/little brother has become close. Never forget that God heals, restores and builds relationships even when we may think it will never happen.

I came from a family of three brothers with me as the baby. My oldest brother was a half-brother and was born to my father and his first wife (that I never knew).

I was born into the Bob and Margaret Clark clan which included my brothers Joe, Bill and myself.

My brother Joe was born four and a half years earlier than myself, and was my big brother. Today we enjoy each other but it was not always that way. In 1964 I graduated from High School and went into the Army and Joe graduated from California State University at Long Beach with a Bachelor's Degree in Education. In 1967 a Master's Degree and in 1973 he completed his Doctorate at the University of Southern California (USC). His life educational journey was from Teacher, Principal, Assistant Superintendent, and Superintendent. During his climb up the educational ladder, alcohol was part of his life. The alcohol became a greater influence until 1990. During the years that I just wrote about, my brother Joe traveled down his path and of course I was going down mine. There wasn't much in common, and our commitments to our lifestyle and our proximity to each other grew more distant. He lived in Southern California and I in Northern California and Oregon (1964 to 1990). During these years our Dad died (1981) and Mom followed in 1984. The years were filled with educational accomplishments, marriage and a daughter. They were also filled with challenges that caused the melt down.

In 1968 my wife and I moved north out of the Los Angeles area to Oxnard. There I involved myself in the Coffee Shop Ministry where kids came off the street into our Coffee Shop, which we called the "Candle Shop". We would provide a setting of coffee, cookies and share God's Word. As kids came off the street and found a new life in Christ, that led to a home that Pam and I opened up for these kids off the street.

I didn't know what I was doing but I became available to God as He was training me both in Bible College and out of College. Life in the training field was a value in "whatever your hands find to do, do with all your might.*

Looking back from my early days of surrender I wanted to work with people needing Jesus. My heart for the hurting was used by God to teach others. Jesus told us "freely you have received freely give".** The Oxnard experience in the Coffee Shop and on the street catapulted me to Bethany Bible College (now Bethany University) in Santa Cruz. In Santa Cruz, my outside college experience, from 1972 this 1974, was as Youth Pastor at Cabrillo Assembly of God. In 1974 I graduated from Bethany College with a Bachelor of Science Degree with a threefold major of Bible, Theology, and Religious Education. At the ripe old

* Ecclesiastes 9:10

** Matthew 10:8

age of 28 Pam and I moved to Oregon and expanded our ministry to the field of Education.

Finding myself in 1974 as a 28-year-old I became part of a larger church with a pastoral staff of six Pastors. As Education Pastor I led a Christian Education Staff of around 60 workers. Over the next two years the Educational Staff grew to approximately 120. I enjoyed this new learning and serving experience. Eugene was the home of Eugene Bible College which was an Open Bible Church College. They hired me to teach Educational Classes. I accepted their offer and taught several classes that related to the educational function in the church.

My next Pastoral experience was moving to Medford to become the Church Administrator. My function was to oversee multiple aspects of the Church. Again I was working with Pastor Reece. I worked as his Youth Pastor back in Santa Cruz. He assigned me to oversee the Youth, Education, Boys and Girls Clubs. I also managed some property purchases and sales. I was learning by doing.

It seems that most learn and then do. Not me! I seemed to be thrust into positions and then learned the secrets of success in those areas.

Next on my journey was a move to Marysville, California to assume my first Senior Pastor function. The next 10 years found me in the Marysville, Yuba City, Arbuckle, and Berry Creek areas.

I Pastored, became Principal and Head Teacher at several Christian schools.

Looking back I continued to see how each move added a different dimension to my life experience. In each new experience came an added love for people, as God continued to "set me up" for my today ministry. Many times I hear individuals tell about how they want to help people that have walked through the dysfunction that they have (or are walking in). It seems to me that our life experience that are "God breathed" makes a difference in the life of others as we walk in obedience over the years, not just months.

I never did drugs but God has used me to help the "druggie". I was never a prison inmate but God is allowed me to make a difference in the incarcerated. How can this be? Looking back it is because of surrender. Looking back it is because of consistency. Jesus said no one who has taken hold of the plow and looks back is fit for the Kingdom of God*.

I'm still looking forward. With my spiritual ears I can hear God say "well done thou good and faithful servant". I've said it before and I will say it again here – I want to finish the race.

There will be no "I almost finished the race". Today I see a mustard seed begin to grow. That mustard seed had a desire, in my heart, to touch people.

In 1976 Pam and I took yet another first. In our move to Medford Oregon, at age 30, our first daughter came into our life. To this point we had been unsuccessful in having children and God blessed us with our first adoption.

In 1978, February 7, our first daughter Tammy arrived via the Medford Airport. As new parents and as a new Staff Pastor we began a new adventure of being the Administrator Pastor at a church. I didn't know about either, being a Daddy was a first, being an Administrator (in charge of a church) was a first.

My past was moving on and God was providing me with yet another experience. Over the next 10 years there were many Pastoral experiences. Our second adoption, was a son and became a Frederick Junior. He was born in 1980. Our third adoption was a daughter. Her name is Melody and she has two daughters named Harmony and Symphony. Isn't that interesting!!! Her two sons are Landon and Jonah. Three weeks later we received Joseph, our fourth adopted from Seoul, Korea.

In this period of time I began substitute teaching in the Public School and started my first Christian School, where I became the Principal and Head Teacher as well as being the Church Pastor. More new firsts! I really didn't know how to be a Principal but I learned by doing. At this point in my life I believe that I was functioning out of my gift of administration even though I was unaware that I had that gift inside of me. God gives us gifts as He wills[*]. This gift helped me to succeed.

Looking back I can see how God used my substitute teaching to lead me to getting a Teaching Credential in the State of California. It didn't appear to me to be

---

[*] I Corinthians 12:11

anything more than just a means to employment that allowed me to pay the bills, as I continued to do the work of a Minister of the Gospel and grew in love for people and a desire to make a difference in the lives of people. I moved into my 40s with four children growing up, Pastoring and operating a Christian School.

In 1988 I was asked to Pastor a Church and Principal the Church School in Berry Creek, California. This mountain community above Oroville was a wonderful experience.

Another new experience came into my life. The Ministry of Teen Challenge. Teen Challenge, a wonderful ministry to men and women with substance abuse and other life controlling experiences, invited me to become involved. I did. Birthed from this involvement was a center known as the Feather River Teen Challenge Center. I became the Board President and became involved with men who were being "set free" from their addictions.

Looking back, this helped to prepare me for the next "big event" in my life. In 1993, while Pastoring being a Principal and Head Teacher in Berry Creek, God spoke a word of direction to me. This wasn't the first time. In 1964, some 30 years earlier God spoke a word of direction that sent my life into the direction of ministry.

The Bible tells us, "My sheep hear My voice and they know Me"*. I do not think it is strange to hear our Lord

---

* John 10:27

speak to us. Samuel heard** the Lord and he was told to respond "here I am". Peter saw a vision and heard instruction from "on high". The Apostle Paul fell to the ground and said "Lord what would You have me to do".*** In every encounter with God there is always a needed response. God never speaks to His creation without wanting a response. Our Father never wastes His time with "Small Talk". I don't think monologue is His style. He speaks. Then He listens, as He has directional conversation with those He is waiting for a response. In 1964 as He called me to serve Him full time, as a 17-year-old, I either had to say yes or no. When he opened doors of ministry, I either had to say yes or no and walk through the door or respond with the "I don't think so, God".

In almost every directional conversation with my Lord, in my 53 years of walking with him(to this time) I didn't have the know how but I had a passion to be obedient to God knowing that the "well done" will never be substituted with an "almost well done" or a "you almost finished the race" or a "you almost obeyed me". I've concluded that all this "My sheep hear My Voice" stuff is not rocket science but a simple lamb following the Shepherd. In all of this it has been fun. It has been a learning experience. I think about the process of figuring it out only to be at the end of the race. The experiences learned on the track of

---

** I Samuel 3:9

*** Acts 9:7

life can be reduced to "not just hearers of the Word but also doers.[*]

Back to the big event of 1993 at the age of 47. I was Pastoring in Berry Creek, Principaling in a Christian School, working with the Feather River Teen Challenge Ministry and God spoke a directional moment into my life. I have always believed that we have a "walk" with Christ. It consists of curves and bends, uphill and downhill, fun times and not so fun times, hurtful situations and blessed situations but is only one walk.

From my surrender in that Study Hall Classroom in April 1964, I have only been on one journey with Christ. At the 1993 point in the journey I had the Lord speak to me to "go teach at a prison".

This directional conversation was unique. In my past God directed me in areas of familiarity. I was a youth ministering to youth. I was a teacher teaching. But prison? I didn't even know where prisons were located. I didn't know that they taught inmates in prison. I assume they just "locked them up" until they let them out.

I had never been in prison or jail. I'd never had a family member or friend in prison (that I know of), But God said "go teach at a prison". I heard God. It wasn't a bad burp or a pizza dream. It was a directional conversation from God to me. It required a response. My response was easy. It was"okay God, I will do that". I didn't know how, as usual, when or where. But I knew God's voice. I have

---

[*] James 1:22

learned over the past years, on my walk, that God never asked us to do something that we are unable to do with His help. I believe whom the Lord calls, He equipes.

Had the Lord equipped me for this? I believe He had. As I look back to the early years of Street Evangelism, Coffee Shop Ministry, the first attempts of living with those who had addictions and then Teen Challenge, this began to prepare me for this part of my walk with Him.

How would I teach at a prison? That is what God said to do.

With my "okay God, I'll do that". I began this section of my journey trying to figure out the "how to" of God's plan.

Someone suggested I call Sacramento at the Department of Corrections. I did. I asked "do you have teachers teaching in the prisons?" Their response was "yes". I then asked "what is required to teach at a prison?" Their response was "you need a California Teachings Credential". I had one of those. A few years earlier I had returned to college and worked on my fifth year studies and obtained a teaching credential. I wasn't sure why I walked this way but God did and I marvel at His knowledge of what is needed in our lives. The next question on the phone was "what else does one have to do to teach at a prison? I was told that I would have to apply for a teaching position. "How do I do that?" I asked. The person continued by telling me I would have to fill out an application and submit it. I said "how do I get an application?" The answer was simple, they would mail me one.

The rest is the process that went on for nearly 3 years.

IT WAS ON.

On June 1, 1996 I was a teacher at Salinas Valley State Prison at Soledad, California, a Maximum-Security Prison, (a level 4 Prison) walking in obedience to the direction of God in my life but still not knowing the why of this direction. Yet knowing that I had heard the Shepherd's voice and having confidence in His knowledge of what is best for me.

From the "go teach at a prison" in 1993 until June 1, 1996 there were some significant events in my life that began to expose me to prison and inmates. My first prison experience was when I became involved in a jail ministry in Atwater, California. A small group of men did services at the jail and also at the Susanville Prison. I was invited to go with them to a service at Susanville. I went. That was my first awakening to the prison culture. I never thought that I would spend many years in the future dedicated to the incarcerated. I don't remember much about that service but I do know that it was a seed planted and remain there until it began to grow.

My phone rang – the voice began to tell me of a crime that was going to send him to prison, He would begin a sentence in just a few days. I cried like a baby. The reality was that this was happening. Day after day I would walk the aisles of the Church and prayed for my friend and his family. I had a hard time believing this happened, but it did. The seed planted in Susanville was growing.

My older brother Joe during this time was teaching at the Prison in San Luis Obispo, California. He had previously been the Superintendent of the Educational Program at Etascadero State Hospital for about 10 years. From time to time we would talk about his experience inside the walls at San Luis Obispo's Men's Colony. My seed grew some more.

I waited. I tested. I pondered the future that was before me.

All I knew was that God said go teach at a prison. The new construction of several prisons unbeknown by me, had begun across the State of California. Completed in 1995 – 1996 I waited as my seed was growing. Then in 1996

I was offered a job as a Teacher at Salinas Valley State Prison at Soledad, California. What did this all mean? I didn't know.

I did know that God spoke to me and then on June 1, 1996, I walked into Salinas Valley State Prison as a Teacher and as an undercover missionary to a world I knew almost nothing about.

CHAPTER THREE

AT AGE FIFTY
PRISON FOR LIFE

I have been walking with the Lord for 33 years and each year has its own history. Collectively the years have their own history. The years of my 50s have been special as I know that God uses this season in life to prepare for the seasons that lie ahead.

3

Actually, I was not yet 50 years old when I walked into Salinas Valley State Prison for the first time. I was only 49 1/2! Lots of years had passed since that April, 1964 surrender in the Study Hall Classroom. It had been 32 years of life experience. Each one a teaching experience and of being mentored by the Lord.

It had been three years since the Lord spoke to me to "go teach at a prison". Those five words I heard clearly. My obedience to that calling was clear. My understanding of the future was not. I guess that is where faith kicks in. Why a teacher at a prison? Because God said so.

I guess it is a little like Jonah. God said go to Nineveh. The difference of the point of calling was Jonah said no and I said yes. The really good part is that I didn't have to face a rocking boat and a great fish's stomach.

I remember the first day at Salinas Valley State Prison. I was still wondering the "why" of being a teacher of academic subjects of math, language arts, science, social studies, spelling, and writing skills. After the first week of orientation, I was introduced to my empty classroom. This newly opened prison had began receiving inmates in the "A Yard" and "B Yard" was next. I was assigned to open up the class on "B Yard", which would be the ABE I Class.

The next week was used to collect books, prepare lesson plans, observe "A Yard" classes and then set up my own class. The class size was 27 students with one student clerk for 5 1/2 hours per day, Monday through Friday. The opportunity to observe other classes on the "A Yard" side was extremely valuable because I had no reference to this type of class that included 27 inmates. There were three other classes in the hall where I taught. This educational location also included an Officer who was always present in the building when classes were in session. I was given a personal alarm and had to carry a wistle.

I don't remember the first class day or second or third. The days became weeks, then months, then years. Every day was different. I enjoyed my 10 years. All the Academic Teachers came from other prisons or from the Public School System. I treated each student with "worth" regardless of their crime and length of sentence. The Prison was a Level 4 – Maximum-Security Prison. Each man having a sentence from a few years to life sentences without parole(LWOP). I had a class with a variety of personalities. Each class also had an assigned clerk.

I had several Educational Clerks, over the years. I had one clerk for about seven years. He had become a Christian but walked away from that belief years after I retired. I am no longer in contact with him although for many years we wrote after I left the prison employment.

One early event was when I discovered the Chaplain at the Prison was an Assemblies of God Minister. I also being an Ordained Assemblies of God Minister, lined me up for the missionary part of my 10 years. Chaplain Doug Moon allowed me to teach weekly Chapel Services. Every week the Chapel would fill with men (around 100 in attendance) who wanted to be there. I believe many lives were changed as the Gospel invaded their spiritual man. Not only did I conduct weekly Chapel (Bible Studies) but once a month, on Sunday, I would speak at three Chapel Services, each on a different yard.

At the weekly Bible Studies I conducted, I would complete my work day, as a Teacher, turn in my class keys and "CHIT out" (the term used for a round metal looking coin that would be given in exchange for a key) the Chapel keys and open up the Chapel. Between weekly Chapel Bible studies and the Sunday Chapel services, I ministered to thousands of men over the 10 years and hundreds of men stood and made commitments to Christ.

One event I will share is about David. On a Friday afternoon Bible Study in the Chapel, at the conclusion of a service, an inmate approached me in the front of the Chapel. As I looked at him and he looked at me he began with the words "we are connected". These words startled me as I looked at him and was trying to figure out what he was saying. He said these words again "we are connected". I was wondering if I had been his Teacher. Maybe he had been in one of my Educational Classes. Although only seconds had gone by and I was processing what he meant. He then said to me "you don't get it do you?". I responded, "no". David then said "you were my Sunday School Teacher and my Royal Ranger Commander". I was looking at him not having a clue due to the fact that it had been 30 years prior and I asked him what his name was. He said "David Michicci". David's brother had been in the youth group that I had leadership in. As we talked, my recollection began to focus. At that time David was about 11 years old. We only talked a little as recall followed Chapel but in that short conversation he added "Pastor I have 14 years. I guess I should have listened to you the first time". My response to David was "you're right you should have". David and I had a few conversations going forward and he was transferred to another Prison. I began a 14 year written relationship with David. He is out now in California, doing parole. There is a lot more to this event but I place it in my history because from this came an emphasis truth in my ministry that speaks truth into the reality of life that says "the decisions I made yesterday will effect my today. And the decisions I make today will effect my tomorrow". The 14 years of David's prison time he walked it out with God and still is.

There was another David, too. This David was released while I was still teaching. I remember saying he would never return to prison. Within a couple years he received some new charges and I believe received eight years more in prison. This was one of the heartbreaks I experienced. I had projected David to be the perfect Resident Director for The Shepherd's Ministry Home. David's mother who was up in years, I think in the 80s, and when he returned for another hitch his Mom passed away and instead of being there for those last years he was locked up again. Until he was sentence I would drive weekly to visit him, while he was still in jail. I would drive over an hour to visit him and spent probably an hour visiting him. After the sentence and the shame settled in he broke off our communication. I have not heard from him since.

There are many stories over the 10 years of my 50s. I couldn't tell them all nor can I remember them all. It was during this period of time that God would fashion my remaining years. Little did I know that God was preparing me for the journey involving inmates both on the inside and the outside.

Many will preach to the inmates but few seem to be willing to invite them into their home or give them their address, or introduce them to their family.

I don't remember if it was the first Christmas or not, but I was leaving my yard after finishing a Chapel Service and I got to the gate where I would buzz the Guardhouse to unlock the passage gate to get out of the B yard area and I just began to weep (hard cry) – I was going home and they were not. That was the beginning of a realization that I had a heart for the prisoner.

I think loving those you work with is a necessity to becoming one with them. I couldn't become one with them by experience. I had never been in prison or had I involved myself in crime, but here I was and I was receiving a love for the man behind the walls.

I just thought God said to teach at a prison but it was what He didn't say that began to work a plan in my life that passed into my 60 years and into my 70s.

In the years at Salinas Valley State Prison stuff happened. We began to travel to Oregon to meet friends for fishing vacations (Central Oregon Area). At age 42 on one of these trips we fell in love with Oregon. Pam and I decided to purchase some land thinking we could retire in this area someday. We had not accumulated much over our years of marriage due to the fact that my pay compensation for ministry was modest. In fact Pam had to work in order for us to meet the obligations of living. We decided if we were ever going to have something, now was the time to get started.

Of course this was God and not because of the fish! We found 5 acres of wooded property in LaPine. In fact to get to our parcel we had to put our tires on the deer trail and the bitter brush scraped the bottom of the car. Five acres – $10,500. We borrowed $3,000 on a Credit Card and the seller carried $7,000 on a note. Each year we would take our tax returns and a few days of vacation to make improvements on the land. First it was electricity, then a well, then a septic tank. **IT WAS ON.**

Somewhere around the year 2000 God began to speak into my heart that there was something more He had in mind than just my teaching math, science, english, and doing Chapel Services and Bible Studies. It wasn't clear but I knew it was happening. Then it came – "I want you to open up a home for men coming out of prison". My response was "how do I do that"? Direction came and his plan continued in a forward motion. That became the 60 years of my life.

Pam and I had been traveling back and forth to Oregon. We would vacation and work on our 5 acres. The children would pull Bitter Brush to make a driveway into the interior of the property. We decided on the location that we would build a house. Drove in corner stakes and "**it was on**". Lots of dirt. The Children didn't like the dirt with no water but we found the Little Deschutes River was a good bathtub. As we were preparing this property we had no idea it would become the cornerstone of The Shepherd's Ministry.

Teaching at the prison, back-and-forth to LaPine, Oregon, Pastoring a church plant in San Juan Bautista and listening to God as he was speaking future things into my heart. It became clear that God spoke to me to open up a home for men coming out of prison. I was seven years into my time at Salinas Valley State Prison. During this time I also planted a Church in San Juan Batista.

The Church in San Juan Batista was a rented bank building that was being used for a storage of shopping carts, tables and other miscellaneous items. This became our Church. I was the only church with a bank vault!!! We used it as a Sunday School Class Room. I walked the community looking for people. I found Johnny. Johnny was a bipolar man that made us his Church. Johnny would sit on the front row – slept a lot and became my friend. There was Norma. Norma pushed her shopping cart to the Church and brought it inside because she didn't want anyone to steal things from her cart. Norma was faithful and like Johnny – she became my friend. The Church also consisted of others that came from the community as well as my son and daughter who began to attend. I Pastored this Church until 2006 when we left for Oregon.

When God spoke to me to open up a home for men coming out of prison there were only two answers. Either yes or no. I am sitting with 40 years of walking with the Lord and I don't ever remember a "no". I do remember responding to the Lord and saying "I can do that". Then followed my next statement "how do I do that?". As with most first things I had never done this before nor did I know anyone who had.

How would you know what to do? How would you know how to do this? God was orchestrating both what to do and how to do it. All of this came over the last three years of my Salinas Valley State Prison experience. When I think back at the stirring of my heart concerning something else God had in mind for me and my journey, I am amazed as to how God can speak quietly into our hearts.

I went on an exploratory trip to Oregon. A journey that would pass this future through the Council of highly trusted brothers in Christ.

I met with an acquaintance in Bend. He was involved in Jail and Prison Ministry. His encouragement to proceed was received and I moved on to the city of Boring, Oregon where I met with Rance my Pastor friend of many years. In our time together he encouraged me to "go for it" that God would go before me. Then I traveled to the Willamette Valley to my longest known Pastor and friend,

Lloyd. In the past I had worked with him as a Youth Pastor, Education Pastor and Church Administrator. These positions were in Churches where he had Pastored. His counsel was "Fred, you can do it". With an encouraged faith and knowing this task was not a crazy task, I headed back to California to continue pondering this new direction. There still loomed the what to do and how to do it.

It happened as I was driving home, I received a phone call from a person who I'd only met once about three years earlier. He came to a Chapel Service at Salinas Valley State Prison accompanied by a lady who had been a honky-tonk piano player and dance hall singer in her past life. What a testimony of a changed life! Jim also shared a little of his life as a past drug user and drug seller and now a Christian. I finish the Chapel with my sermon. Now I'm on my way home to California from Oregon after my exploratory trip and Jim is on the phone. He remembered me from that Chapel Day and wanted to talk with me about Prison Ministry. I got home that evening and the next day Jim and I met for coffee.

The next day the conversation was about Jim opening a home for men coming out of Prison. We talked and I shared with Jim how God had spoken to me to do the same thing and I was returning from Oregon. What a God thing this was!

Jim wanted me to help him as he developed his program. He had scheduled a man with experience in this kind of ministry to come out from Illinois to meet with us and explain his ministry. We spent two days with Manny and I begin to write a manual that would become the foundation of The Shepherd's Ministry.

From the purchase of our 5 acres and taking several years to build the house, I was able to purchase several homes that were repossessed homes. One of the larger homes became the home called "The Shepherd's Inn".

In early 2006 I gave the renters a notice to move so I could begin the preparation of getting the house ready for the first Resident. I didn't have anyone to bring into the home but in my heart I remember God saying to open up a home for men coming out of Prison and that was that. The rest was active faith of that which was yet to come.

I believe that the men coming out of Prison deserved a good place to live. A clean place to live. A safe place to live. A Godly place to live. The house for the ones that God would send needed fresh paint, new carpet, good beds, good furniture, good curriculum and good almost everything!

In 2004 at age 57 the unexpected happened. While working at Salinas Valley State Prison I had an heart attack. This event ushered in a new adventure in my life. My life's activities would change. God's plan did not. Over the next 2 1/2 years events happen that created the fulfillment of opening up a home for the men coming out of Prison. Over the next months I received 3 stints in my heart. That required time off from work.

I would return to work and then be off work because of my heart. Off work and back to work. Finally a fourth stint. During this time God began to put His final touches on my move to Oregon to open up a home for men coming out of Prison. It was in this time that all of the manuals, bylaws, brochures the what to do and how to do it came into existence. I had hours and spent hours preparing for the next adventure in my life.

In October, 2005 I was directed to return to work with a Doctor's Release or I could not return. At this point in time my Doctor would not okay me to return. As my 10 years of employment was coming up, it seemed best to take my 10 year retirement option. I received a retirement of $1,000 a month with $600 coming out for my share of medical insurance. With my $400 a month in hand – I followed God's plan. Over the next six months I was involved in getting things ready in Oregon and wondering how the finances would cover such a plan of a home for men coming out of Prison. In June 2006 we were fully ready for the first resident in our home. Still with just $400 in hand but having years of knowing that God provides for those whom He calls. I knew that God loved the man coming out of prison more than I did. With that faith we just trusted in God. Miracle after miracle took place that provided for the plan that God had prepared for us.

Jumping ahead in time – in June, our last Sunday at our Church in San Juan Batista, who had a going away dinner for us - with car, truck and trailer full, we headed to Oregon. Pam pulling the trailer and with me driving the car – we headed towards Weed, California. At Weed, Pam headed to LaPine, Oregon on Highway 97 and I continued up I-5 and was headed to Santiam Correctional Institution (SCI) to pick up our first resident, Wade. Our moto was "Meet Me At The Gate" and so it was on that June day of 2006.

"IT WAS ON"

CHAPTER FOUR

AT AGE SIXTY
" I'M RETIRED"

These years are filled with a whole bunch of new things. The physical challenges will lead in to the spiritual victories. That is how God does things. In fact He does exceedingly, abundantly, above all that we ask or even think.

4

"It was on". I'm retired. I moved in with Wade. Pam moved into our retirement home. I didn't have a Resident Director yet so I became the Resident Director and also the Ministry Director. Wade was worth it. My obedience to God was worth it.

I picked up Wade on Monday morning after driving most of the night in order to get to Salem. I picked him up "At The Gate" and we drove across the mountain to LaPine.

In Sisters, we stopped and met with his mother at the hamburger place in town. That was an exciting moment as a son who had just got out of prison was now eating with his mother. She was thrilled that he had found Christ in Prison and had a home to go to that was a Discipleship Home. Needless to say that first day was a long day but was worth the loss of sleep. Obedience to the plan of the Lord is always worth it.

I had scheduled a preaching service to share The Shepherd's Ministry Program and Wade found himself in Church on that first Sunday out of Prison sharing how God had set him up to be in The Shepherd's Ministry Program. That was a great service.

I met Wade as a result of his sister and her husband being in the carpet business. In April 2006 when I was able to get the rented home back I began the task of painting and carpeting. The carpet folks, which I knew, came over to the house to measure the floor for the new installation of carpet. The next day I went into their shop to select a carpet color and explained what I was doing with this house. I discovered that she had a brother who was imprisoned. She told me how he had been writing letters that appeared to be indicating that he had a "born-again experience". I explained our program to her and told her that I would bring a brochure and some other material to her the next day and she could send it to her brother. That brother was Wade and he became our first residence at The Shepherd's Inn.

I believe to this day that God saw Wade when he called me to open up a home for men coming out of Prison. That is the great love that God bestows upon us.

Several other residents were received. In about four months a Resident Director was found and I returned to live in my retirement home with Pam. I traveled daily from my house to The Shepherd's Inn to eat breakfast, pray and conduct the studies for the morning and spend the day with the residents of the home. Each afternoon we worked in the community.

In the middle of June, while living in The Shepherd's Inn, I received mail which was extremely welcomed. Due to my heart attack happening on the grounds of the State Prison at Soledad I was awarded a Workmen's Compensation judgment stating that my heart attack was related to my work. Now instead of Insurance and $400 a month in cash, I received a lifelong award under a Medical Disability because of the damage to my heart. My income included full Medical Provision for anything related to my heart and a Suplimental Insurance for the rest. My cash grew from $400 to "enough". I knew God would take care of this !!! In addition, I began receiving individual contributions to The Shepherd's Ministry. Two such gifts have continued monthly as they partner with us in this ministry to inmates. Frank and Susan, and Mike have never missed giving a monthly gift to us from the beginning. God is faithful to His promise that tells us that when we give it will be given unto us. The women at Prineville Assembly of God blessed us with Quilts that fit each of our beds. What a blessing that was.

In October of that year I received a call from one of the District Officers in the Oregon Assembly of God office. Pastor Bob asked me if I had any openings on Sunday to fill the pulpit in Paisley. I had begun back in June speaking wherever I could concerning The Shepherd's Ministry. I would take the men with me as we presented our Ministry. My calendar was full. The first Sunday Services I was able to schedule in Paisley were the first two Sundays in December. We went. The men and I shared The Shepherd's Ministry. During that time we also had two granddaughters living with us as their mother was in Iraq.

We took two cars, traveled through a snowstorm and had a good time. At the second Sunday I seem to have "fallen in love" with these "Paisley folks". Again, **IT WAS ON".**

My calendar for services in 2007 had not been made. I did have one in January and one week in February and one in March. I called Pastor Bob and told him I would schedule the next weeks ahead and fill in my calendar with the dates that I had available. I didn't know that this would turn into a nine-year Pastoring experience. After all I am retired !!!

So now I'm retired, Director of The Shepherd's Ministry and Pastor of Paisley Assembly of God. Each trip to Paisley was 105 miles each way. My 60s would walk out in this manner.

The years were filled with a daily routine of eating to-gether, praying together, studying together, working to-gether as a family. The Shepherd's Ministry provided an opportunity for men to become "Men of God" in an en-vironment that was created for that purpose. I wanted to invest in the lives of men coming out of prison. Each man that we picked up "At the gate" usually came to us with just one bag in his possession. Almost all had no money. But money wasn't the issue as I had decided that there would be no cost to this ministry and that I would assume the financial responsibilities of it all. I had acquired the faith that God would provide. Some provision was early and others just on time. Never has it been late. A checking account was created and the monies, that were donated to the ministry would be placed into this account. We also placed the honorariums from the Churches in which we spoke into this account. All of this was about faith and the fact that God had spoken His desire for there to be a home for men coming out of prison.

Would they really walk out faith in Christ? Would the Shepherd's Ministry really make a difference. Could a structured environment make a man into "a" man of God"?

The years have proved that only the man that surrenders his will to God's Will, continues to be the faithful man of God.

From the beginning I knew my desire was not to be a Transitional House or a Half-Way House. I saw Transitional Housing as a temporary place to stay and hang out. I never fought against this concept but it wasn't my idea of a achieving the best for the man I was giving my resources to. I wanted their housing to be their home. We rehearsed that many times. Another big issue to me was that we were not a "Half-Way House" but a "Whole-Way House". I have known several Half-Way Houses and it seemed that there was something better than that. I wanted The Shepherd's Ministry Inn to be a "Whole-Way" house.

As mentioned earlier in this book, I talked about my early concept that God wanted for all of us – to have a whole surrender. Not a halfway or partial surrender. I wanted a Whole-Way House for the men to become a Whole-Way man of God. My goal was to show them how. Did I always act whole myself? My heart was. But sometimes I missed the mark. I got frustrated over an action of a man or when a man left the home. I have always wanted to finish this race with God facing off with me – eyeball to eyeball – with the well done thou good and faithful servant.

Early on I knew that the men I would be trying to help and mentor had to come to an understanding that there must be a change in a man's "playground, playmates and playthings" if lasting relationship with God was to prevail. Without changes in these areas I didn't think a man could have a substantial change. I still believe this to be true. In almost all cases of failure, I see the man returning to either his playground or playmates or playthings. That's why Jesus told us that there was an element for success called "leaving all".

As the years of my 60s rolled along The Shepherd's Ministry was established with men that came and some of those exited before they graduated. The first resident, Wade, graduated in December 2007 after 18 months of the program. We had a great celebration. It came in the form of a graduation followed by a fellowship party at one of our local Churches. He received graduation gifts of tools and other gifts and was the focus of a lot of love expressions from the local Church and others who supported our Ministry. Wade had never been celebrated like this before. He was overwhelmed by the fact that he had made it this time. He completed the program. He was still on target with becoming a Man of God. Wade stayed on at the house. Helped in the Supervisory role and eventually became the Resident Director.

Today Wade is married and faithfully works in a local gas station and continues to call Pam "Mom" when he sees her at his work site. Today we are friends.

As with any ministry there were joys and disappointments. The old saying "you can lead a horse to water but you can't make him drink" was certainly at play in our Ministry. Disappointments were few but nevertheless stressful and in every case followed by many tears. I knew every time a man walked away it was like cutting the rope to a life buoy. Their best hope was severed. I always prayed that somehow or somewhere the departing Resident would find the end of the cut rope and be rescued.

Another successful story is Cecil. We picked Cecil up "At the gate". Cecil was our youngest. He had served less time in prison than most of our residents but had given his heart to Lord and was determined to never return to Prison. Most of his family had experienced incarceration and he landed in Prison following in the path of family members. In his conversion he came to a decision to follow Christ and to break the curse of his family lifestyles. The family exception was a grandmother who loved and prayed for him. Cecil although younger than the other Residents applied himself to the programs prayer, study, and work ethics. The decisions he made affected his days ahead. He graduated in 2009 with $2,000 in a savings account and a belief that he was breaking the family curse of criminality in his family. As of the writing of this chapter Cecil is married. Has one child and the curse remains broken.

In 2010 I traveled to Cogayon de Oro, Philippines for three weeks. The Shepherd's Ministry appeared to be running well and I decided to take the invitation from Pastor Elpedio Tabacloan and make this trip.The missionary trip was exciting and profitable. Years before I traveled on another missionary trip to Vladivostok, Russia.

All missionary trips have been an addition to my journey. The results of the Philippine trip was a church built and named Miracle Assembly of God. The funds for this Church came from the LaPine Assembly of God, Paisley Assembly of God and The Shepherd's Ministry.

Pam and I traveled to Guatemala for the first time in October, 2012. Two more trips were made over the next years. We worked with the missionary, Darren and Heidi Walker. They are Assembly of God Missionaries working with the Latin America Child Care Program. Pam and I traveled throughout Guatemala doing missionary work alongside Missionary Walker. Our third trip to Guatemala was in October, 2015. Each trip consisted of many miles and many locations. We probably know more about the Guatemalan countryside than most Guatemalans. Each trip was scheduled with preaching opportunities throughout the country.

Annually I am tested for my heart condition. In May, 2011 I was informed that I needed an Aortic Heart Valve replacement. I underwent open-heart surgery and they replaced the Aortic Valve with a Pig Valve. That's right – a Pig Valve. I have a variety of jokes about having a Pig Valve inside of me. As long as it keeps "oinking" I'm doing ok. About eight months later they added a Pacemaker to my chest. I continue my journey with some unusual parts but continue to believe that my life is in His hands and as long as I have breath. I want to be poured out.

Our Family

Family has been a part of my life. Although there are many miles between some of the family, we continue to be family. Each unit is it's own.

Our oldest daughter Tammy is in the Army as an Warrant Officer and has two girls. Kaisha is currently attending the University of Alabama and Kamille is about to graduate from High School.

Fred Jr. lives on 5 acres next door to ours. He and Liz have provided four wonderful grandchildren for our pleasure(most of the time). Their names are Ryan, Nolan, Mason, and Holly.

Melody, our youngest daughter, and Derek have added four more kids to our flock. They are Harmony, Landon, Jonah, and Symphony. That totals 10 grandchildren altogether.

There is a sad part in our family. Our fourth adopted son Joseph, Korean born, decided when he was 16, that home was not the place for him. His gay lifestyle was not compatible to our belief system. He sought refuge with those who spoke into his heart differently than we did. From that day, when he ran away from home, I have not seen him. At age 32 he passed away in Southern California living like he chose to live.

My commitment to Christ and my desire to follow Him, did not shelter me from this family pain. Yet in all of it, God was with us.

I have a middle brother, who I haven't mentioned yet, that is two years older than I. His name is Bill and he is living in Ranier, Oregon, with his wife Gilda. They have two sons. He retired from Mobil Oil years ago.

My most precious family person is Pam. She is not only my most favorite person but when we go to the Prison together, the men in the chapel, love Pam, too. When I gave my heart to the Lord in 1964 Pam and I went to the same church. At that time, I knew Pam was in love with me. In the sovereignty of the Lord, He knew the importance of a great wife that could keep me in line. On July 9, 1965 we were married and that has continued to this day. We plan to finish our journey together working with the inmates. As you read this book you can figure out how many years we've been married. It has been a "bunch"!!!

I want to mention my parents. My Dad had been an alcoholic prior to my birth in the family. Joe and Bill, my older brothers, mentioned earlier, also were born after our Dad became a Christian. The life of my Mom and Dad were lives of loving the Lord and taking us to Church. They were parents that raised us to follow in the steps of the Christian Faith. They were in love with the Lord to the end. Dad went to be with the Lord first and Mom followed a few years later. It has been years since they passed away but the memory of Godly parent remain with me.

I have come to the end of my 60s. I'm still on the move. At the end of 2015 I retired from the Paisley Church.

CHAPTER FIVE

AT AGE SEVENTY AND BEYOND "IT IS STILL ON"

When you are busy it is hard to get or be lazy. The years that lie ahead, no matter what they bring, God wants us to be faithful to the end. That's my goal.

5

"IT IS STILL ON"! If you are reading this book and it is 2018 and beyond I am still on the journey either here or in Heaven. My journey is an Eternal Journey as it will end one day on earth and continue in Heaven. Life for all of us never really ends. It only changes location. One of the motivating Scripture statements for my life has been "Fulfill Your Ministry".* I am still being poured out because that is God's plan. There are events in my journey that are not written, not because they were not important, but it may be that there are too many events to put in this book or they are currently being lived out.

I am retired for the second time as I write this last chapter. I approach age 71. Weekly I drive to Deer Ridge Correctional Institution, in Madras, where I teach a

---

* 2 Timothy 4:5

Mentoring Class and one Chapel Service a month. I also have a Mid-Week Chapel Service, too.

About 10 months ago I requested to begin a mentoring class that allows me to teach a few men before their release. My goal is to mentor them in the ways of the Lord. As they release I am allowed to follow them on the outside, if they want. This arrangement is the first of it's kind, as I understand it. The first released inmate, Christopher, I picked up "At The Gate", drove him to Eugene and spent two days with him as he settled in. On Sunday, my wife and I returned to Eugene to take him to Church and to plug him in to a Mentor at Willamette Christian Center. When released, the Parolee has to get to the Parole Office and other places to get settled in. If no transportation, it's the bus!

They all need a job. That is not easy. When asked where they have previously lived it's not easy for them to say "I just got out of prison". I have told each man to tell the truth. Some employees will not hire them and others will provide an opportunity for them. The bottom line is that the best proof of integrity will be if they are honest and a good worker. All employers understand that.

As a last chapter is being written, a couple of stories have followed me throughout my journey. The first one goes back to 1968 when I was a Youth Pastor in the City of Manhattan Beach.

The Senior Pastor was on vacation and I received a call at the Church from Sister Gilroy. I didn't know her first name because it was just Sister Gilroy. She asked me to come over because brother Gilroy was dying. I didn't know at the age of 22 how to handle a death bed experience but I did know the Senior Pastor was gone and it was only me left. I traveled to their house.. They had a screen covered porch area with two beds and there was space to walk between them. As I walked into the room brother Gilroy, (I didn't know his first name either because he was just brother Gilroy) was lying in the bed and I walked over to the bedside and stood there gazing down at him. It was different than the battlefield of Vietnam or the Autobahn of Germany when I viewed a dead body. Brother Gilroy nearing death's door but with the spirit of a giant. After a short time of talk, brother Gilroy turned his head toward Sister Gilroy, who was standing on the other side of the bed, and said "Sister Gilroy come on the other side of the bed and lets lay hands on this young preacher".

Sister Gilroy did and **"IT WAS ON"**. A Pentecostal prayer meeting began. The spirit of God prevailed and I left for my trip back to my Church Office on a spiritual cloud. About halfway back to the Church I realized I forgot to pray for brother Gilroy! This event has been embedded into my life. One of brother Gilroy's desires was to pray for this young preacher 50 years ago. On many occasions I have spoke that I want to go out like brother Gilroy, praying for others.

My Dad is another lasting story in my life. At age 72 he had a stroke and was unable to speak, walk or feed himself. He was paralyzed on one side. During the nine months he lived, I prayed for his healing. We visited him as much as we could, as he and Mom lived in Arkansas City, Kansas and we lived in California. On trips there, I would sit with Dad. He always wanted to go to the dayroom of the facilities whenever a Church Group came. They would sing and share the Word. They would sing songs that were familiar songs to the elderly. Songs like "What a friend we have in Jesus", "Amazing Grace" and others. As the songs rang through the room it reached the heart of my Dad and he would begin to cry "crocodile tears". As Jesus flooded his heart, tears rolled down his face. He was having communion with the One who had carried him out of his alcoholism.

My Dad was a house painter and I also remember the times that I would go to work with him and he would be painting while listening to a Christian Station on the radio. It was either someone preaching a message or Christian Music. He would be on the ladder and having his own personal Church Service and "crocodile tears" would be running down his cheek. My Dad was in love with Jesus to the end. I have prayed "Lord let me go out like my Dad loving you to the end".

Prison is a lonely place for men. Most are guilty of what has placed them behind the bars. Regardless of that fact it is still lonely. Their closest contact is the next bunk. The man in line to the dining room. The man sitting at the table across from them. The Counselors are assigned many inmates and are not to get too close.

My experience that some Officers(Guards/Cops) are often disrespectful and not very tenderhearted. I understand this because it seems to go with the territory. The inmate is often viewed as just a piece of "poop". No prison could ever be ran without the Officers who show up daily to do their job. Officers become hardened as a result of responses of the inmate. Any statement that a person makes concerning Prison Life will have two sides to it. I thank God for the Officers and their good work and pray for them often.

From the days of teaching, as an Academic Teacher at Salinas Valley State Prison I have tried to view inmates as persons worthy of a respectful encounter. Even when guilty, God forgives those who ask Him for forgiveness. I was guilty when I found forgiveness! My dad said on several occasions, "son, remember the pit from which you where dug".*

Many times it is only the mother or a family member that "really cares" for the prisoner. When a disconnected person is viewed as caring it stands out and hope rises in the heart of the inmate. That is why Jesus talked about visiting those in prison.

I've enjoyed all of the Prisons that I have been able to work in as a Volunteer. During the past 10 years my journey has taken me primarily to three different Oregon Prisons. Snake River Correctional Institution(SRCI) in Ontario, Oregon. Warner Creek Correctional Facility (WCCF) in

---

* Isaiah 51:1

Lakeview, Oregon and Deer Ridge Correctional Institution (DRCI) in Madras, Oregon.

For the past several years I have spent the most time at DRCI in Madras. I have witnessed the graciousness of the staff at DRCI and on many occasions an individual Officer will thank me for my efforts, as I volunteer. Annually they have a Volunteer Appreciation Emphasis that simply says "thank you for your service". I think I don't need a thank you when I'm doing what I want to do, but it is always appreciative to hear the expression of "thank you". The Chaplain and the Inmates also thank me for coming.

My wife and I travel one and a half hours each way to be able to Minister to the men. I thank God for the car that gets me there. For the money to buy our gas and the money to buy lunch or dinner at the Chinese Restaurant,

Jack in the Box, or Taco Bell.

My last Chapter and Beyond may be short or long. It may be that as you are reading this last line

"IT IS STILL ON"!

THE KINGDOM OF GOD IS LIKE...

The Kingdom of God is like a man who looks out at the trees in the woods and sees many trees. One is tall and growing and grandeur. Another is still standing but dead. Others are young and growing.

> **The tall and grandeur tree**: is the believer who has walked with God. Applying the principles of the Kingdom day by day.

> **The dead tree**: is dead. It has become lifeless through a process of non application. Now, just dead. Waiting for the future state of falling over or being cut down and being consumed ahead of time and contrary to its intended use.

The young and growing trees: are alive today and will become like the tall and grandeur tree or like the dead tree. The only way it will maintain its growth pattern is through the process that happens day by day.

All of us find ourselves in this story.

EPILOGUE

The book is ending but the story goes on in the lives of those I have touched. Our labor is never unprofitable as I have heard many times from the incarcerated. At night as they lay their head on their pillow they will remember something that had been said to them from a Mom or a Grandmother or a Pastor or a Friend. I trust in the days ahead there will be those who will recall the guy in Chapel or in the Bible Study or in the Classroom or behind the Pulpit, who believed that he could walk a new life out, with the help of the Lord, to the end.

There is a song in my spirit right now that has the lyrics- "what is this I hear, it's the sound of music. It just goes on". The kingdom of God just goes on and someone with breath will continue to spread the Good News throughout the land.

I always wanted someone who would take over The Shepherd's Ministry and run the program. But it doesn't seem like that will happen (or will it?). God who is the God of now will continue to reach in to the Prisons and touch the lives of those who have an ear to hear and an eye to see.

It was just three days ago, from the writing of this page, as I was going into DRCI, that I thought, I wonder if I were in a wheelchair if they would still let me come and speak to the men. The message is that important. I guess that is why I'm still at it. Retired twice but still not retired. Still saying to God, "I give up". My life doesn't belong to me I have been bought with a price. I gave you that 53 years ago! Let me go out like Brother Gilroy or my Dad believing that lives can be changed by the power of God, and that we make a difference. I am crying.

"IT IS STILL ON"

What about you? You who read this page. You have more to give. You have more to live. What will you do with what you have left? It will not be only what you say but what you do.

Current Add-On

My friend David Miccichi, after eight month of Parole was cut loose from the system. He had five years of Parole. Is that God or what !!!!

.

Made in the USA
Las Vegas, NV
13 July 2023

74584579R00046